BLUES PLAY-ALONG

ok & CD for B♭, E♭, Bass Clef and C instruments

VOLUME 9

PLAY 8 SONGS WITH A
PROFESSIONAL BAND

HOW TO USE THE CD:

Each song has <u>two</u> tracks:

1) Full Stereo Mix

All recorded instruments are present on this track.

2) Split Track

Keyboard and **Bass** parts can be removed
by turning down the volume on the LEFT channel.

Guitar, Horn, and **Harmonica** parts can be removed
by turning down the volume on the RIGHT channel.

Cover photo © Photofest

ISBN 978-1-4234-8707-4

HAL•LEONARD®
CORPORATION

7777 W. BLUEMOUND RD. P.O. BOX 13819 MILWAUKEE, WI 53213

Visit Hal Leonard Online at
www.halleonard.com

ALBERT COLLINS

BOOK

CD

BRICK

WORDS AND MUSIC BY JOHNNIE MORISETTE

INTRO-GUITAR SOLO

FAST SHUFFLE

CHORUS

BRICK, BA - BY, THAT'S WHAT I'M GON-NA THROW UP-SIDE YOUR HEAD.

I SAID, NOW, BRICK, BA - BY, THAT'S WHAT I'M THROW UP-SIDE YOUR HEAD.

YEAH, YOU GOT ME SO WOR - RIED.

Collins' Mix
By Albert Collins

Guitar Solo

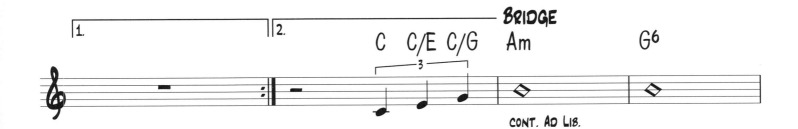

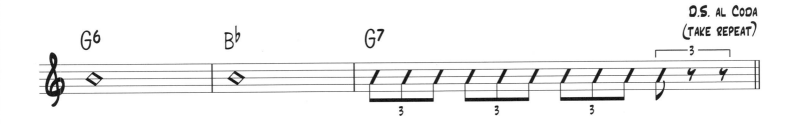

Don't Lose Your Cool
By Albert Collins

Uptempo Swing ♩ = 176

GUITAR/ORGAN/SAX SOLOS

TO CODA ⊕

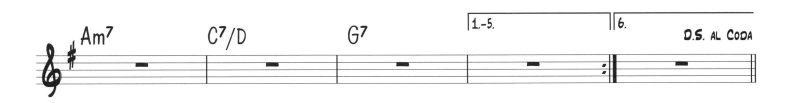

⊕ CODA

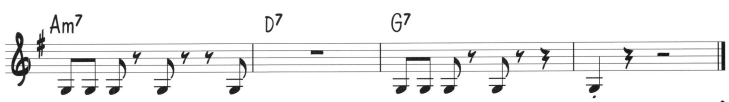

9

Frost Bite
By Albert Collins

Guitar Solo
Medium Fast Rhumba ♩ = 168

10

Frosty

By Albert Collins

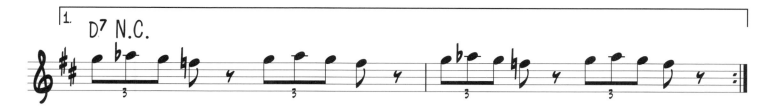

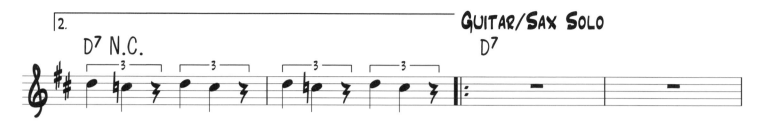

GUITAR/SAX SOLO

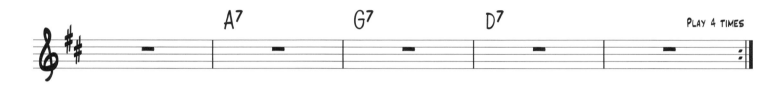

PLAY 4 TIMES

GUITAR SOLO

CODA

D.S. AL CODA

N.C. (D)

(GTR.)

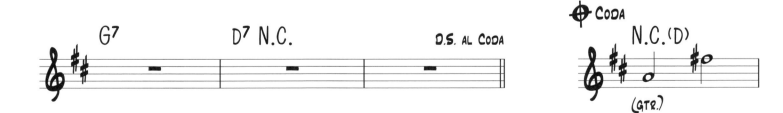

D13

N.C.

I Ain't Drunk

Words and Music by Jimmie Liggins

STAY DRUNK ALL THE TIME. ___

GUITAR SOLO

GUITAR SOLO

OUTRO-GUITAR SOLO

ADDITIONAL LYRICS

2. COME HOME LAST NIGHT, ALL LUSH.
   BABY GET IN A FUSS, I SAID, "HONEY, HUSH."
   I DON'T CARE WHAT THE PEOPLE ARE THINKIN',
   I AIN'T DRUNK, I'M JUST DRINKIN'.

3. YOU DONE THE RIGHT THING, I WANNA THANK YOU, TOO.
   NOW, LET'S HAVE A LITTLE DRINK, JUST ME AND YOU.
   I DON'T CARE WHAT THE PEOPLE ARE THINKIN',
   I AIN'T DRUNK, I'M JUST DRINKIN'.

4. I WANNA TIP YOU BABY BEFORE I GO.
   I'LL BE BACK TOMORROW NIGHT AND DRINK SOME MORE.
   I DON'T CARE WHAT THE PEOPLE ARE THINKIN',
   I AIN'T DRUNK, I'M JUST DRINKIN'.

Additional Lyrics

2. I said, "Did you get your dresses?" She said, "Yes, one or two.
But I had to get me some shoes, and I need some jewelry, too."
She had two hundred dollar dresses that I could've made and I can't sew.
Fifty dollar pair of shoes, and I thought, "You so and so."
I said, "What about the jewelry?" as calmly as I could.
She said, "Honey, you will love them, they are pure African wood."

C Version

Trash Talkin'
Words and Music by Albert Collins

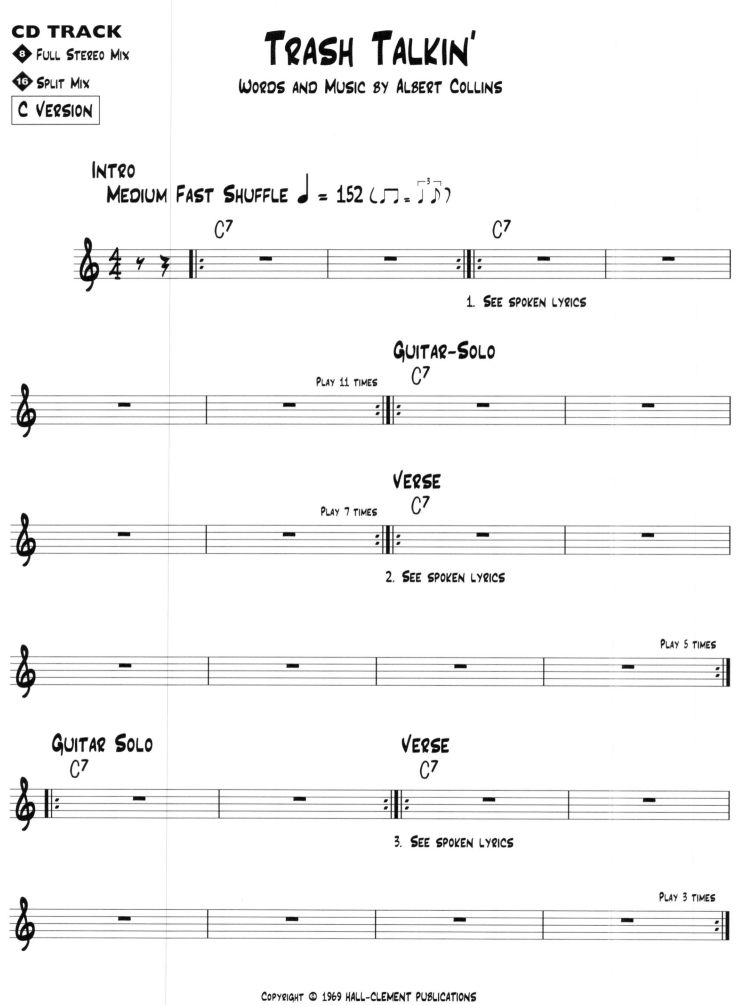

Intro
Medium Fast Shuffle ♩ = 152

1. See spoken lyrics

Guitar-Solo
Play 11 times

2. See spoken lyrics

Play 5 times

Guitar Solo   **Verse**

3. See spoken lyrics

Play 3 times

Outro-Guitar Solo

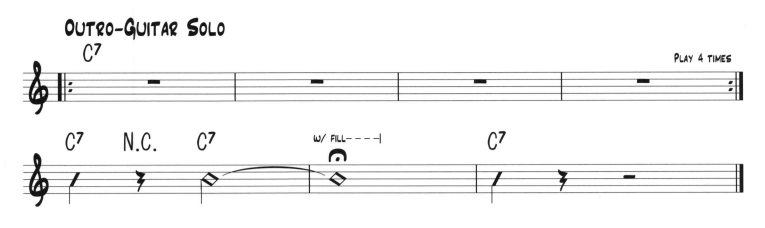

Spoken Lyrics
Verse 1

Spoken:

I went down to Albert's Alley, to pick up on me a Collins Mix. I went down to the bar and ordered me a drink,
and tried to relax myself.
Looked around and saw two soul sisters.
They were sippin' soda.
Another look caught their companion, on the dance floor,
they were doin' the Collins Shuffle.
Pretty soon a cute little number came and asked me to do the Stump Poker with her.
I told her I couldn't do the Stump Poker,
I could show her how to do the Sissy.
We were on the dance floor and I was doin' my thing.
After a while, out of nowhere, up walks her boyfriend,
while she's standing there doin' the shivers and shake.
He gave me a look that was very icy blue,
and believe me, he made me thaw out.
I said to myself, "Albert,
don't lose your cool."

Verse 2

Spoken:

By this time I'd gotten hungry, 'cause I smelled someone
cookin' catfish. Ordered me some along with some greens,
told him definitely I didn't want no leftovers. Cook took so
long about fixin' my grub, I had to go see what was takin'
him so long. He back there jivin', had to tell him to get it
together. He asked me, "Can't you wait?" Made me mad.
I said, "No man, I ain't got time. I got to keep on
pushin', got to make it down the soul road, gotta go do some
turnin' on."

Verse 3

Spoken:

Don't want for us to get me no dyin' flu, so I'm leavin' town,
goin' home. I got homesick anyway. I'm leavin' this place
before I freeze, goin' home to defrost. Ain't gonna have me
lookin' like a snow cone. I don't know, it's getting rough.

Brick

Words and Music by Johnnie Morisette

Intro-Guitar Solo
Fast Shuffle ♩ = 176

Chorus

Brick, ba-by, that's what I'm gon-na throw up-side your head.

I said, now, brick, ba-by, that's what I'm throw up-side your head.

Yeah, you got me so wor-ried.

COLLINS' MIX

BY ALBERT COLLINS

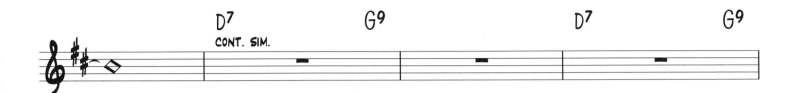

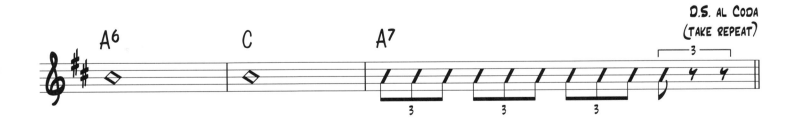

Don't Lose Your Cool

By Albert Collins

Uptempo Swing ♩ = 176

GUITAR/ORGAN/SAX SOLOS

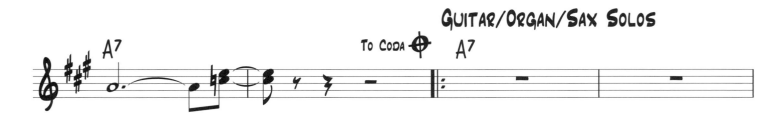

Frost Bite

By Albert Collins

Guitar Solo
Medium Fast Rhumba ♩ = 168

SAX SOLO

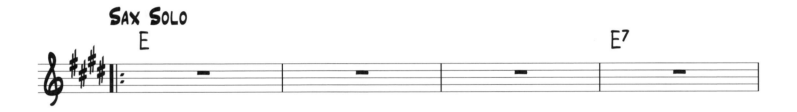

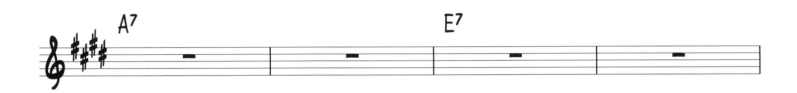

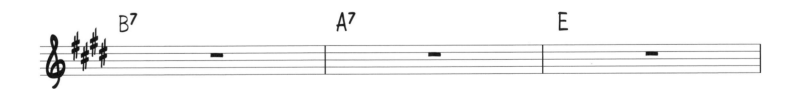

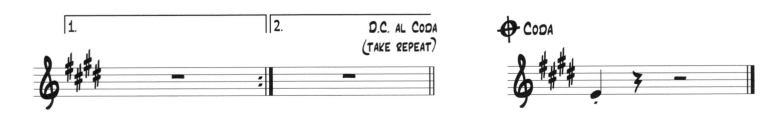

Frosty

By Albert Collins

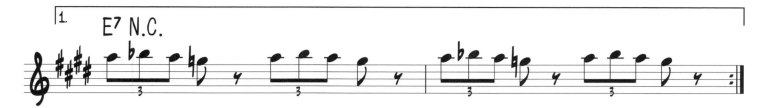

GUITAR/SAX SOLO

PLAY 4 TIMES

GUITAR SOLO

D.S. AL CODA

CODA

(GTR.)

STAY DRUNK ALL THE TIME. ___

ADDITIONAL LYRICS

2. COME HOME LAST NIGHT, ALL LUSH.
   BABY GET IN A FUSS, I SAID, "HONEY, HUSH."
   I DON'T CARE WHAT THE PEOPLE ARE THINKIN',
   I AIN'T DRUNK, I'M JUST DRINKIN'.

3. YOU DONE THE RIGHT THING, I WANNA THANK YOU, TOO.
   NOW, LET'S HAVE A LITTLE DRINK, JUST ME AND YOU.
   I DON'T CARE WHAT THE PEOPLE ARE THINKIN',
   I AIN'T DRUNK, I'M JUST DRINKIN'.

4. I WANNA TIP YOU BABY BEFORE I GO.
   I'LL BE BACK TOMORROW NIGHT AND DRINK SOME MORE.
   I DON'T CARE WHAT THE PEOPLE ARE THINKIN',
   I AIN'T DRUNK, I'M JUST DRINKIN'.

CHARGE. A BANK-A-MER-I-CARD. MAS-TER CHARGE.

MAS-TER CHARGE. A BANK-A-MER-I-CARD. 2. I SAID.

GUITAR SOLO

VERSE

3. "THEY WERE TWO HUN-DRED DOL-LARS AND I PAID

ONE AND A HALF." I JUST DID-N'T BE-LIEVE IT. SO, MAN, I JUST HAD TO LAUGH. I COULD

SEE IT IN MY MIND, ON A HORSE LIKE PAUL RE-VERE. I HATE TO

CHECK MY MAIL-BOX 'CAUSE THESE BILLS KEEP COM-IN' HERE. MAS-TER CHARGE.

OUTRO-GUITAR SOLO
w/ VOC. AD LIB

REPEAT AND FADE

ADDITIONAL LYRICS

2. I SAID, "DID YOU GET YOUR DRESSES?" SHE SAID, "YES, ONE OR TWO.
BUT I HAD TO GET ME SOME SHOES, AND I NEED SOME JEWELRY, TOO."
SHE HAD TWO HUNDRED DOLLAR DRESSES THAT I COULD'VE MADE AND I CAN'T SEW.
FIFTY DOLLAR PAIR OF SHOES, AND I THOUGHT, "YOU SO AND SO."
I SAID, "WHAT ABOUT THE JEWELRY?" AS CALMLY AS I COULD.
SHE SAID, "HONEY, YOU WILL LOVE THEM, THEY ARE PURE AFRICAN WOOD."

CD TRACK

8 Full Stereo Mix
16 Split Mix

Bb Version

Trash Talkin'

Words and Music by Albert Collins

Outro-Guitar Solo

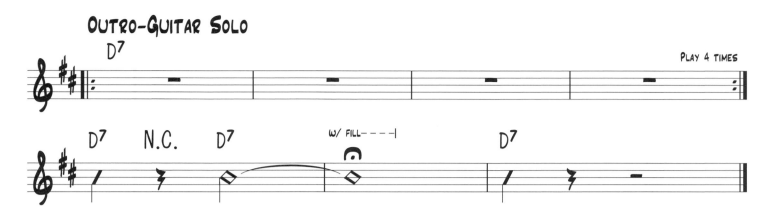

Spoken Lyrics

Verse 1

Spoken:

I went down to Albert's Alley, to pick up on me a Collins Mix. I went down to the bar and ordered me a drink, and tried to relax myself.
Looked around and saw two soul sisters,
they were sippin' soda.
Another look caught their companion, on the dance floor,
they were doin' the Collins Shuffle.
Pretty soon a cute little number came and asked me to do the Stump Poker with her.
I told her I couldn't do the Stump Poker,
I could show her how to do the Sissy.
We were on the dance floor and I was doin' my thing.
After a while, out of nowhere, up walks her boyfriend,
while she's standing there doin' the shivers and shake.
He gave me a look that was very icy blue,
and believe me, he made me thaw out.
I said to myself, "Albert,
don't lose your cool."

Verse 2

Spoken:

By this time I'd gotten hungry, 'cause I smelled someone
cookin' catfish. Ordered me some along with some greens,
told him definitely I didn't want no leftovers. Cook took so
long about fixin' my grub, I had to go see what was takin'
him so long. He back there jivin', had to tell him to get it
together. He asked me, "Can't you wait?" Made me mad.
I said, "No man, I ain't got time. I got to keep on
pushin', got to make it down the soul road, gotta go do some
turnin' on."

Verse 3

Spoken:

Don't want for us to get me no dyin' flu, so I'm leavin' town,
goin' home, I got homesick anyway. I'm leavin' this place
before I freeze, goin' home to defrost. Ain't gonna have me
lookin' like a snow cone. I don't know, it's getting rough.

Brick
Words and Music by Johnnie Morisette

GOT ME TALK-IN' _____ OUT OF MY HEAD.   YEAH, YOU

VERSE

KNOW I _____ LOVE YOU,   AND YOU KNOW __ MY LOVE IS TRUE.   WELL,

I CAN'T UN-DER-STAND IT, BA - BY, _____ THE WAY YOU TREAT ME LIKE YOU _____ DO. __

I'M GON-NA CHUCK A BRICK, BA - BY.   I'M GOIN' CHUCK A BRICK AT YOU. __

GUITAR SOLO

To Coda

1.   2.

I GOT A

D.S. AL CODA
(TAKE REPEAT)

CHORUS

BRICK, BA - BY,   AND I'M GOIN' THROW UP-SIDE YOUR HEAD. __   I SAID, NOW,

Coda

37

Collins' Mix

By Albert Collins

GUITAR SOLO

BRIDGE

CONT. AD LIB.

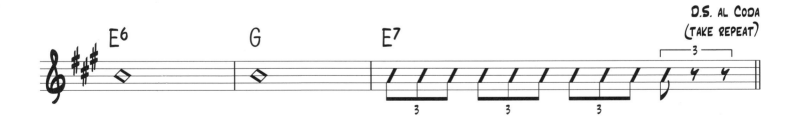

D.S. AL CODA
(TAKE REPEAT)

Don't Lose Your Cool

By Albert Collins

Uptempo Swing ♩ = 176

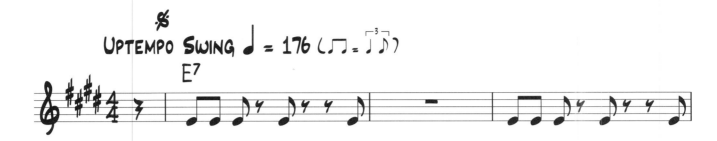

E7

Guitar/Organ/Sax Solos

To Coda ⊕   E7

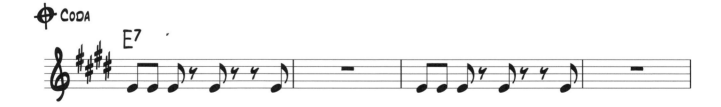

A7   E7

F#m7   A7/B   E7   1.–5.   6.
D.S. al Coda

⊕ Coda

E7

A7   E7

F#m7   B7   E7

CD TRACK
◆ 4 Full Stereo Mix
◆ 12 Split Mix

Eb Version

Frost Bite
By Albert Collins

Guitar Solo
Medium Fast Rhumba ♩ = 168

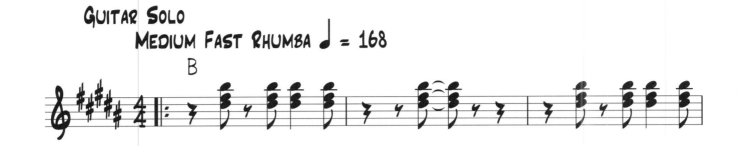

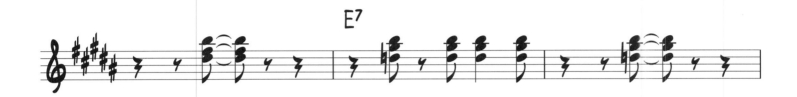

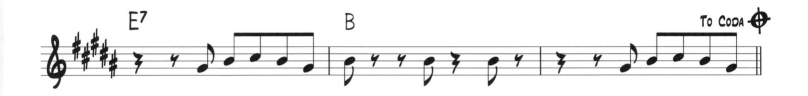

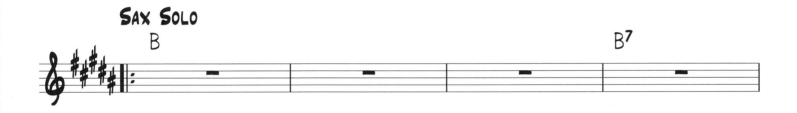

SAX SOLO

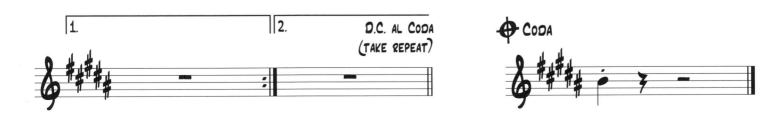

Eb Version

Frosty

By Albert Collins

Fast Shuffle ♩ = 168

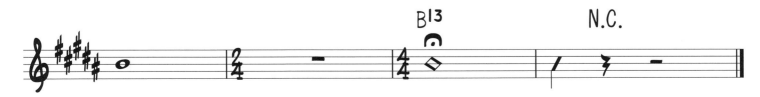

I Ain't Drunk

Words and Music by Jimmie Liggins

STAY DRUNK ALL THE TIME. ____

Additional Lyrics

2. Come home last night, all lush.
   Baby get in a fuss, I said, "Honey, hush."
   I don't care what the people are thinkin',
   I ain't drunk, I'm just drinkin'.

3. You done the right thing, I wanna thank you, too.
   Now, let's have a little drink, just me and you.
   I don't care what the people are thinkin',
   I ain't drunk, I'm just drinkin'.

4. I wanna tip you baby before I go.
   I'll be back tomorrow night and drink some more.
   I don't care what the people are thinkin',
   I ain't drunk, I'm just drinkin'.

Master Charge

By Gwendolyn Collins

CD TRACK
7 Full Stereo Mix
15 Split Mix

Eb Version

Intro-Solo
Moderate Funk ♩ = 100

1. My

wife has a charge card ___ that I got her the oth-er day. ___ I owe

2. See additional lyrics

five hun-dred dol - lars that's just for yes-ter-day. I said, "Hon-ey, here's a pre-sent. Go

out and shop a-round. Get a cou-ple of dress-es and browse a-round ___ down-town." She

did just what I told ___ her. Bought one, two, or three, ___ then came home look-in' sil-ly mak-in'

𝄉 Chorus

goo-goo eyes ___ at me. Mas-ter Charge. ___ Mas-ter Charge, a Bank-a-mer-i-card. ___

Mas-ter Charge. ___ Mas-ter

Additional Lyrics

2. I said, "Did you get your dresses?" She said, "Yes, one or two.
But I had to get me some shoes, and I need some jewelry, too."
She had two hundred dollar dresses that I could've made and I can't sew.
Fifty dollar pair of shoes, and I thought, "You so and so."
I said, "What about the jewelry?" as calmly as I could.
She said, "Honey, you will love them, they are pure African wood."

Trash Talkin'
Words and Music by Albert Collins

Intro
Medium Fast Shuffle ♩ = 152

A7   A7

1. See spoken lyrics

Guitar-Solo
A7
Play 11 times

Verse
A7
Play 7 times

2. See spoken lyrics

Play 5 times

Guitar Solo   Verse
A7   A7

3. See spoken lyrics

Play 3 times

Outro-Guitar Solo

Play 4 times

Spoken Lyrics

Verse 1

Spoken:

I went down to Albert's Alley, to pick up on me a Collins Mix. I went down to the bar and ordered me a drink, and tried to relax myself.
Looked around and saw two soul sisters.
They were sippin' soda.
Another look caught their companion, on the dance floor,
They were doin' the Collins Shuffle.
Pretty soon a cute little number came and asked me to do the Stump Poker with her.
I told her I couldn't do the Stump Poker,
I could show her how to do the Sissy.
We were on the dance floor and I was doin' my thing.
After a while, out of nowhere, up walks her boyfriend,
while she's standing there doin' the shivers and shake.
He gave me a look that was very icy blue,
and believe me, he made me thaw out.
I said to myself, "Albert,
don't lose your cool."

Verse 2

Spoken:

By this time I'd gotten hungry, 'cause I smelled someone
cookin' catfish. Ordered me some along with some greens,
told him definitely I didn't want no leftovers. Cook took so
long about fixin' my grub, I had to go see what was takin'
him so long. He back there jivin', had to tell him to get it
together. He asked me, "Can't you wait?" Made me mad.
I said, "No man. I ain't got time. I got to keep on
pushin', got to make it down the soul road, gotta go do some
turnin' on."

Verse 3

Spoken:

Don't want for us to get me no dyin' flu, so I'm leavin' town,
goin' home. I got homesick anyway. I'm leavin' this place
before I freeze, goin' home to defrost. Ain't gonna have me
lookin' like a snow cone. I don't know, it's getting rough.

Brick

Words and Music by Johnnie Morisette

GOT ME TALK-IN' ___ OUT OF MY HEAD. YEAH, YOU

Verse

KNOW I ___ LOVE YOU. AND YOU KNOW ___ MY LOVE IS TRUE. WELL,

I CAN'T UN-DER-STAND IT, BA - BY, ___ THE WAY YOU TREAT ME LIKE YOU ___ DO. ___

I'M GON - NA CHUCK A BRICK, BA - BY I'M GOIN' CHUCK A BRICK AT YOU. ___

Guitar Solo

I GOT A

Chorus

D.S. AL CODA
(TAKE REPEAT)

BRICK, BA - BY, AND I'M GOIN' THROW UP-SIDE YOUR HEAD. ___ I SAID, NOW,

Collins' Mix

By Albert Collins

Guitar Solo

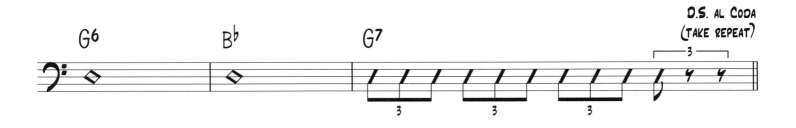

Don't Lose Your Cool

By Albert Collins

Guitar/Organ/Sax Solos

Frost Bite
By Albert Collins

Guitar Solo
Medium Fast Rhumba ♩ = 168

SAX SOLO

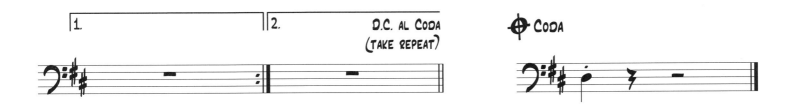

🎷 C Version

Frosty
By Albert Collins

I Ain't Drunk

Words and Music by Jimmie Liggins

STAY DRUNK ALL THE TIME. ____

Additional Lyrics

2. Come home last night, all lush.
   Baby get in a fuss, I said, "Honey, hush."
   I don't care what the people are thinkin',
   I ain't drunk, I'm just drinkin'.

3. You done the right thing, I wanna thank you, too.
   Now, let's have a little drink, just me and you.
   I don't care what the people are thinkin',
   I ain't drunk, I'm just drinkin'.

4. I wanna tip you baby before I go.
   I'll be back tomorrow night and drink some more.
   I don't care what the people are thinkin',
   I ain't drunk, I'm just drinkin'.

Additional Lyrics

2. I said, "Did you get your dresses?" She said, "Yes, one or two.
But I had to get me some shoes, and I need some jewelry, too."
She had two hundred dollar dresses that I could've made and I can't sew.
Fifty dollar pair of shoes, and I thought, "You so and so."
I said, "What about the jewelry?" as calmly as I could.
She said, "Honey, you will love them, they are pure African wood."

Trash Talkin'
Words and Music by Albert Collins

Outro-Guitar Solo

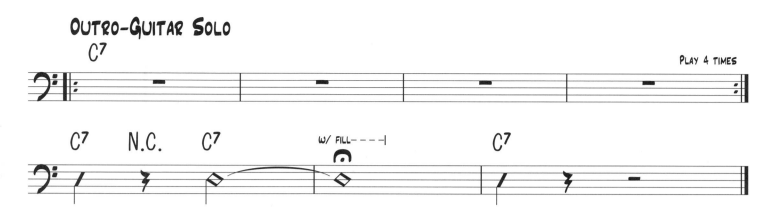

Spoken Lyrics

Verse 1

Spoken:

I went down to Albert's Alley, to pick up on me a Collins Mix. I went down to the bar and ordered me a drink, and tried to relax myself.
Looked around and saw two soul sisters, they were sippin' soda.
Another look caught their companion, on the dance floor, they were doin' the Collins Shuffle.
Pretty soon a cute little number came and asked me to do the Stump Poker with her.
I told her I couldn't do the Stump Poker, I could show her how to do the Sissy.
We were on the dance floor and I was doin' my thing.
After a while, out of nowhere, up walks her boyfriend, while she's standing there doin' the shivers and shake.
He gave me a look that was very icy blue, and believe me, he made me thaw out.
I said to myself, "Albert, don't lose your cool."

Verse 2

Spoken:

By this time I'd gotten hungry, 'cause I smelled someone cookin' catfish. Ordered me some along with some greens, told him definitely I didn't want no leftovers. Cook took so long about fixin' my grub, I had to go see what was takin' him so long. He back there jivin', had to tell him to get it together. He asked me, "Can't you wait?" Made me mad.
I said, "No man, I ain't got time. I got to keep on pushin', got to make it down the soul road, gotta go do some turnin' on."

Verse 3

Spoken:

Don't want for us to get me no dyin' flu, so I'm leavin' town, goin' home. I got homesick anyway. I'm leavin' this place before I freeze, goin' home to defrost. Ain't gonna have me lookin' like a snow cone. I don't know, it's getting rough.